4/13

THE DAYTONA 500

by Dustin Long

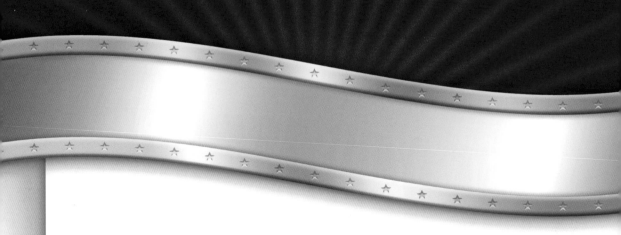

Printed in the United States of America,
North Mankato, Minnesota
102012
012013

 THIS BOOK CONTAINS AT LEAST 10% RECYCLED MATERIALS.

Editor: Chrös McDougall
Series Designer: Craig Hinton

Photo Credits: Chris O'Meara/AP Images, Cover, Title; Glenn Smith/AP Images, 5; Alex Menendez/AP Images, 9, 11, 59 (bottom); Bettemann/Corbis/AP Images, 13, 20, 57, 60 (bottom); ISC Archives/Getty Images, 15, 27, 58 (top); AP Images, 17, 18, 25, 59 (top left); RacingOne/Getty Images, 23, 59 (top right); RIC FELD/AP Images, 29, 31; Robert Alexander/Getty Images, 33; PRYOR/AP Images, 36; David Graham/AP Images, 38; Roger Simms/AP Images, 40, 58 (bottom left); Phelan Ebenhack/AP Images, 43; Jamie Squire/Getty Images, 46; Reed Saxon/AP Images, 49; David Graham/AP Images, 51; The Daytona Beach News-Journal/Kelly Jordan/AP Images, 53, 58 (bottom right); Terry Renna/AP Images, 60 (top, left); Scott A. Miller/AP Images, 60 (top, right)

Cataloging-in-Publication Data
Long, Dustin.
 The Daytona 500 / Dustin Long.
  p. cm. -- (Sports' great championships)
Includes bibliographical references and index.
ISBN 978-1-61783-669-5
1. Daytona 500 (Automobile race)--Juvenile literature. 2. Stock car racing--Juvenile literature. I. Title.
796.72/06/875921--dc22

2012946242

TABLE OF CONTENTS

Young Gun

Ten days before he drove in his first Daytona 500, Trevor Bayne said he was not nervous. He was excited.

"Since I was five years old, I wanted to be here at this point," Bayne said, standing just outside Daytona International Speedway. "Now that we're here, I think we're going to try to make that statement that we're . . . here to stay."

Those were lofty words for a teenager. He would not celebrate his twentieth birthday until the day before the 2011 Daytona 500—the

Trevor Bayne leads Carl Edwards, David Gilliland, and Bobby Labonte to the checkered flag on the final lap of the 2011 Daytona 500.

A Family Affair

Various families have played a major role in **NASCAR**'s development over the years. When Trevor Bayne won the 2011 Daytona 500, he drove for the Wood Brothers. Glen Wood started the racing team in 1950. Wood's brothers soon began helping him, and that is how the team got its name. The team went on to win many races and revolutionize pit stops in **NASCAR**.

Bayne's victory marked the fifth Daytona 500 win for the Wood Brothers. Many of the most successful drivers in **NASCAR** history have raced for the Wood Brothers. For all that he did in racing from his role as a driver and car owner, Glen Wood was inducted to the **NASCAR Hall of Fame** in 2012. His brother, Leonard, was selected to the 2013 Hall of Fame class. Glen's sons, Eddie and Len Wood, and daughter Kim Hall now run the team.

biggest race of the National Association for Stock Car Auto Racing (NASCAR) season.

Since the first Daytona 500 in 1959, only 34 men had won the race before that sunny February day in 2011. The winners included many of NASCAR's greatest drivers. Richard Petty, Dale Earnhardt Sr., and Jeff Gordon each won the race at least once. Petty won it a record seven times.

The Daytona 500 also has created some of NASCAR's most memorable moments. There have been last-lap crashes and side-by-side finishes. Cars often race inches apart while going nearly 200 mph (322 km/h).

The finish of the first Daytona 500 was so close that it took three days to determine the winner.

The race has also become known for its spectacular crashes. Cars have flipped, tumbled, and rolled over. Often several cars have crashed together, sending smoke rising and sparks flying. One race even ended with two drivers fighting. Another time, a driver climbed back into his car and drove away after it rolled over.

It is such action that draws fans to Daytona Beach, Florida, each February for what is called the "Great American Race." They come to watch the best stock car drivers in the world. More than 175,000 fans pack the grandstands and millions more watch on television.

For Bayne to prove he belonged, he would have to make it to the end of 200 laps. That is never easy on Daytona's 2.5-mile (4-km) tri-oval.

Race On

Two cars hit 30 laps into the 2011 Daytona 500. They spun and crashed. Then more cars spun and crashed. When the smoke cleared, 14 cars were damaged. Bayne's car, though, was ahead of the accident. He avoided trouble, just as he would the rest of the day.

The action was intense throughout the race. The lead changed a record 74 times. And toward the end of the race, Bayne was at the front.

Bayne led when the white flag waved, signifying the race's final lap. Three cars were lined up behind him. He later admitted thinking that, if nothing else, he could say he led the Daytona 500 with one lap to go.

He figured the cars behind would gang up on him and pass him on that final lap around the speedway. As the cars exited Turn 2, two more cars joined the battle. The top six cars all raced nose to tail. Bayne led, but it appeared it would be only a matter of seconds before he would be passed.

Bayne still led in Turn 3. Exiting Turn 4, the final turn, the battle changed. Two cars fell back. It was down to four cars for the win. They

Green-White-Checkered

The 2011 Daytona 500 was scheduled to go 200 laps. It actually ended after 208 laps. There was no mistake, though. In 2004, NASCAR changed its rules. If a caution flag waved just before the end of the race, NASCAR would attempt to finish the race without a caution. It is NASCAR's version of overtime. Bayne won on the second attempt to finish without a caution. Many refer to the rule as a green-white-checkered. The name is for the flags used during a race. The green flag starts the race, the white flag signals the final lap, and the checkered flag ends every race.

Jamie McMurray leads the pack down the front stretch at the 2011 Daytona 500. The Daytona 500 is known as the "Great American Race."

maneuvered behind Bayne. But no one could pass him. As Bayne's car crossed the finish line, he became the Daytona 500's youngest winner. He was 20 years and one day old.

"Are you kidding me?" Bayne said on his radio to his team after crossing the finish line.

Finding Victory Lane

Shocked that he won, Bayne had to call his team on his in-car radio and ask how to get to Victory Lane, where winners of every race go.

Before he went, though, he took his red-and-white No. 21 car and drove it through the grass along the track's frontstretch. He spun his car around, doing donuts. After stopping in the grass, his team ran to him.

"Look at this celebration," Darrell Waltrip, a former Daytona 500 winner, said on Fox's broadcast of the race. "This is unbelievable. This is fairy-tale stuff. This is like once upon a time."

A smiling Bayne climbed out of his car and stood atop the door, facing thousands of cheering fans. He raised his index finger as he fell back into his crew. They carried him on their shoulders. After they let him down, he got back into the car and drove to Victory Lane.

When he climbed out of his car in Victory Lane, multi-colored confetti rained on him and his Wood Brothers racing team. "I keep thinking I'm dreaming," he said.

A New Star

Trevor Bayne began racing when he was five years old. Success came quickly for the Knoxville, Tennessee, native. He raced go-karts for eight years and won three world championships and 18 state and track championships. He also won more than 300 feature races. Bayne worked his way through various racing series. He was the youngest rookie of the year in two different series. He made his debut in NASCAR's Nationwide Series at age 18. That series is a level just below the Sprint Cup Series. He made his Sprint Cup Series debut at age 19. He won the Daytona 500 in only his second career Sprint Cup Series start.

Trevor Bayne celebrates with his teammates in Victory Lane after winning the 2011 Daytona 500.

Celebration

The fun was just beginning. The morning after his victory, he flew to ESPN's studios in Connecticut and appeared on the network throughout the day. Then it was off to Chicago and later San Francisco and Hollywood. He also received a phone call from the Vice President of the United States, congratulating him on his victory. A friend on a mission trip in India sent Bayne a text message with a photo of children holding a banner that read: "Good job, Trevor. We're proud."

Everybody knew who Trevor Bayne was. He was a Daytona 500 champion.

Beach to Speedway

Humans have always wanted to go as fast as possible. They ran to see who was the fastest. They raced horses to see who could go faster. And when cars were invented, humans again wanted to go faster than anyone else.

Daytona Beach, Florida, once was the home to those who wanted to go fast. It is why the city hosts the Daytona 500.

Racing began in the area in 1903 in Ormond Beach, Florida. It is located just north of Daytona Beach. Two men decided to see who had

Cars such as this six-cylinder Ford racer competed on the hard sand at Daytona Beach and nearby Ormond Beach during the early 1900s.

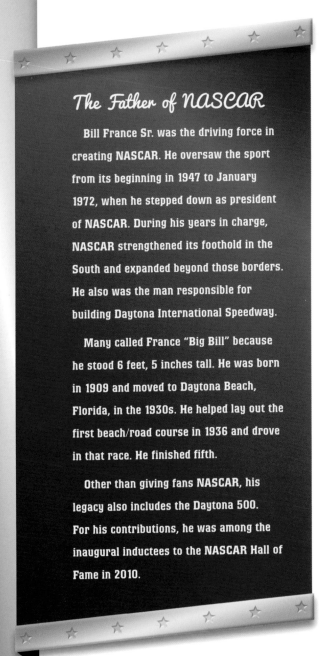

The Father of NASCAR

Bill France Sr. was the driving force in creating NASCAR. He oversaw the sport from its beginning in 1947 to January 1972, when he stepped down as president of NASCAR. During his years in charge, NASCAR strengthened its foothold in the South and expanded beyond those borders. He also was the man responsible for building Daytona International Speedway.

Many called France "Big Bill" because he stood 6 feet, 5 inches tall. He was born in 1909 and moved to Daytona Beach, Florida, in the 1930s. He helped lay out the first beach/road course in 1936 and drove in that race. He finished fifth.

Other than giving fans NASCAR, his legacy also includes the Daytona 500. For his contributions, he was among the inaugural inductees to the NASCAR Hall of Fame in 2010.

the fastest horseless carriage. The wide beaches and hard-packed sands created a suitable place to race. Others followed. They raced against the clock. Daytona Beach soon became a place where many came to attempt land speed records. That continued until 1935. By that time, Daytona Beach had earned its nickname of "The Birthplace of Speed."

Stock car racing began on the beach in 1936. Cars raced there until 1958. As more people began to live near the beach, the future of those races became uncertain. A new place would have to be found.

Bill France Sr. competed in that first stock car race on the beach. He quit racing in 1946 and began promoting the races.

Cars race around the track at Daytona International Speedway early in the inaugural Daytona 500 in 1959.

France dreamed of building a large racetrack in Daytona Beach so the cars could race there instead of on the actual beach. The result was Daytona International Speedway.

The speedway opened in 1959. A lap around the track measures 2.5 miles (4 km). The corners are banked 31 degrees, allowing the cars to go very fast. It was a revolutionary racetrack when it debuted.

First Daytona 500

The first Daytona 500 was held that year, in 1959. More than 40,000 people attended the race. Fifty-nine cars competed. It appeared that

Johnny Beauchamp won, but he came across the finish line beside two other cars. Three days later, after officials reviewed newsreel footage and photos of the finish, they determined that Lee Petty had actually crossed the finish line first. Petty was declared the winner. Even then, people were talking about the Daytona 500.

That was only the beginning for this race. The next year also proved significant. Junior Johnson lamented how his car was not as fast as others during practice for the Daytona 500. But he noticed something interesting. When he ran his car right on the rear bumper of another car, he could keep up.

Starting Fields

Today 43 cars start in a NASCAR Sprint Cup race. That was not the case in the sport's early days. The first Daytona 500 in 1959 had a 59-car field. Richard Petty, who went on to have so much success in the event, finished fifty-seventh in 1959. The largest starting field for the Daytona 500 featured 68 cars in 1960. Ned Jarrett, who started that race fifty-fourth, went on to finish sixth, gaining 48 spots. The Daytona 500 has never started fewer than 40 cars through 2012.

Johnson did not understand the dynamics that two cars running nose to tail can go faster than a car alone. But he used it to his advantage and won the 1960 Daytona 500. Soon other drivers learned about the drafting technique Johnson used. It remains a key part of the racing even today.

The Race Rolls On

Just two years after winning the inaugural Daytona 500, Petty had an accident at the track that shortened his career. In 1961, Petty was driving in a qualifying race for the Daytona 500. Another car and Petty's car tangled. They both crashed through the guardrail and rolled in the

Mario Andretti holds up his trophy with his wife by his side after he won the 1967 Daytona 500

air, landing outside the racetrack. Petty spent the next four months in the hospital, all but ending his career.

Petty's son, Richard Petty, had actually crashed through the guardrail and left the track just before. Richard Petty, though, was not injured. In fact, he would go on to become the Daytona 500's most successful driver.

The 1963 Daytona 500 featured a storybook finish. Days before the race, Marvin Panch was injured testing a sports car at the track. His car rolled upside down and caught fire. Many ran to help Panch. A driver named Tiny Lund helped pull Panch out of the car, saving Panch's life. However, Panch was burned and could not compete in the Daytona 500.

The Wood Brothers owned Panch's car. With Panch injured, they decided to put Lund into Panch's car. Lund went on to win that race.

Just three years after a crash sent his car flying out of the track in 1961, Richard Petty won the Daytona 500 for the first time in 1964. Petty led the final 148 laps of the 200-lap event to win. That race featured five drivers who later were inducted into the NASCAR Hall of Fame. Those five were Petty, Johnson, Ned Jarrett, David Pearson, and Cale Yarborough.

Because Daytona was such a big and important race, drivers from other racing series often competed. Mario Andretti, who raced open-wheeled cars in the Indianapolis 500, won the 1967 Daytona 500. He would later win the Indianapolis 500 and a Formula One championship, making him the only driver to win all three.

Fantastic Finish

One of the most memorable finishes in the Daytona 500 came in 1976. Petty and Pearson entered the last lap battling for the victory. They ran side-by-side in Turn 4. Petty's blue-and-red No. 43 car was on the inside. Pearson's red-and-white No. 21 was on the outside.

Then their cars hit as they exited Turn 4. Petty's car swerved. Pearson's car turned and slammed the wall nose first. Then Petty lost control of his

car and smashed into the wall too. They were only a few hundred yards from the finish, but both cars were spinning. Fans stood, yelling and screaming.

Petty's car bounced off the wall. He spun across the track and stopped in the infield grass about 20 yards (13.8 km) from the finish line.

Petty could not restart his car. Pearson's car was farther back, but the engine was still running. So Pearson put his car into gear and slowly drove through the grass toward the finish line. He passed Petty's car and won the race.

"I've never seen anything like that!" exclaimed Jackie Stewart, the analyst on ABC's broadcast of the race.

"Unbelievable!" ABC announcer Bill Fleming said.

Only three years later, the finish of the Daytona 500 would be even more dramatic.

Richard Petty

Richard Petty is simply known as "The King." No driver has ever topped his career total of 200 NASCAR wins or likely ever will. His seven championships are tied for the most in NASCAR history, matched only by Dale Earnhardt Sr. Petty became as well known off the track as he was known for winning. He embraced his role as a star of the sport and is known for his kindness to fans. Stories abound of him staying well after races to sign autographs for every fan that wanted one. Years later, he became known for his trademark cowboy hat and his sunglasses. He joined Bill France Sr. among the inaugural inductees to the NASCAR Hall of Fame in 2010.

Quite the Show

In 1979, people did not have cell phones. The Internet did not exist. Only a few stations were available on television. So when CBS decided to show the Daytona 500 live from start to finish for the first time in the event's history, it was an important moment for the sport.

At the time, there were three major channels on television: ABC, CBS, and NBC. All-sports network ESPN would not debut until later in 1979. There was also no Fox. It would not debut until 1987.

Richard Petty celebrates in Victory Lane after his surprise win at the 1979 Daytona 500.

Showing the Daytona 500 from beginning until end was a gamble by CBS. Auto racing rarely was shown live on television back then. But the gamble proved to be one of the key moments in the growth of the Daytona 500 and NASCAR.

White Out

A snowstorm blanketed part of the United States during the weekend of the Daytona 500. It was considered the worst storm in 57 years in Washington DC. Parts of northern Virginia and Maryland had as much as 20 inches (50.8 cm) of snow. Parts of North Carolina, Delaware, New Jersey, and Pennsylvania received at least 10 inches (25.4 cm) of snow during that weekend.

NASCAR and TV

Television coverage of NASCAR races has come a long way since that 1979 Daytona 500. Today, every NASCAR Sprint Cup race can be seen live on television. However, the Daytona 500 remains the most-watched NASCAR race of the season. Fox broadcast the 2012 Daytona 500 and stated afterward that more than 36.5 million US viewers watched at least a portion of the race. It was the most-watched Daytona 500 ever on Fox.

Forty-one stock cars round the wet track at Daytona International Speedway early in the 1979 Daytona 500.

The weather was just as bad elsewhere. It was so cold that the majority of the five Great Lakes were frozen over for the first time on record.

The snow and cold weather trapped many people in their homes. With only a few channels to watch on television, they had limited options. So many decided to check out the Daytona 500.

Television ratings measure how much of the country watches a particular show. The rating for the 1979 Daytona 500 was higher than any Daytona 500 in the next 23 years.

Those watching saw quite a finish. The 1979 race started slowly—literally. Early-morning rain forced the race to begin under caution because the track was still wet. After 15 laps, the green flag waved and the cars took off. Crashes in the first 75 laps took out some contenders. The intensity grew as the race got closer to the end.

Quite a Ride

Donnie Allison and Cale Yarborough battled for the lead in the final laps. Yarborough had won NASCAR's championship the previous three years. Allison was the younger brother of the legendary Bobby Allison. They were among a few drivers who lived in Alabama and were nicknamed the "Alabama Gang."

Donnie Allison led as he exited Turn 2 on the final lap. Yarborough's car was only a few feet behind. As they rocketed down the backstretch, Yarborough eased his car toward the bottom of the track to pass Allison. He could not. Allison moved his car down the track to block.

They both went farther down the track. The left-side tires of Yarborough's car ran in the grass and mud off the track. Then the cars hit. Allison's car skidded up the track. He fought the steering wheel and tried to keep his car straight. As he did that, Yarborough was doing the same with his car, which was nearly out of control.

They hit again, slamming door to door. Both turned toward the wall in Turn 3. Tires squealed as they slammed on the brakes and tried to slow down. They could not avoid crashing.

Both cars slid down the track's steep banking toward the infield grass. They stopped only a few feet apart. Seconds earlier they were battling to win the race. Now they were done and would not win.

Richard Petty, who was in third place, drove by both to take the lead. He went on to win his sixth Daytona 500. It was as unlikely a victory as Petty ever scored in his career.

Payday

Richard Petty and his team collected $73,900 for winning the 1979 Daytona 500. That figure has jumped tremendously since. Matt Kenseth, who won the 2012 Daytona 500, collected $1,588,887 for himself and his team. Even the second-place finisher in 2012, Dale Earnhardt Jr., collected more than $1 million.

It was not until 1987 that the Daytona 500 winner collected more than $200,000. The first time a Daytona 500 winner collected more than $1 million was in 1998. Dale Earnhardt Sr. won that race and pocketed $1,059,805. Every Daytona 500 winner since has received a check for at least $1 million.

Drivers typically split their race winnings with their team. Depending on how his contract with the team is written, a driver can make about 50 percent of the race earnings if he wins a race.

After making one more trip around the 2.5-mile speedway, Petty headed down pit road. Many of his pit crew members climbed onto the car. Some sat on the hood. Others sat on the trunk. As he slowly made his way to Victory Lane, a fight was breaking out back in Turn 3.

There's a Fight!

Allison and Yarborough yelled at each other. Things did not escalate until Bobby Allison arrived. Bobby stopped to see if Donnie needed a ride back to the garage area. Then Yarborough began yelling at Bobby Allison. The legendary driver yelled back. Yarborough

approached Bobby Allison's car, leaned in through the driver's side window area and took a swing.

Yarborough was upset at Bobby Allison for an incident earlier in the race. Bobby was battling Donnie for the lead with Yarborough third. Bobby Allison tapped his brother's car. That sent Donnie Allison's car spinning and his rear wheels flew off the ground briefly. He skidded down the backstretch and into the muddy infield grass, which had been soaked by the morning rain.

From Point A to Point B

It took 1979 winner Richard Petty 3 hours, 28 minutes, and 22 seconds to complete the 500-mile race. The race's average speed was 143.977 mph (231.7 km/h). If someone just drove 500 miles in a passenger car and averaged 60 mph (96.6 km/h), it would take more than eight hours to cover that distance. The 1980 Daytona 500 remained the fastest race in the event's history through 2012. Buddy Baker needed only 2 hours, 48 minutes, and 55 seconds to run 500 miles. That equates to an average speed of 177.602 mph (285.8 km/h). The variation depends on the number of caution laps that slow the cars while the track is cleared of accidents or debris.

Yarborough also slid through the grass, splashing water high into the air, in that incident. Bobby Allison's car slid through the grass and backed into a berm that was built to keep cars from crashing into the infield lake.

So it was that accident that led to Yarborough confronting Bobby Allison in Turn 3 after the race.

Bobby Allison quickly climbed from his car and the fight began. Yarborough swung his helmet at Bobby Allison. Yarborough then tried to kick at Bobby Allison, who grabbed Yarborough's leg. They both fell to the ground. Safety workers held Donnie Allison back. The workers then separated Yarborough and Bobby Allison.

Fans saw the action as CBS showed the final portions of the fight to the nationwide television audience.

The publicity of that event only grew in the coming days. As time went by, the finish and the fight would be viewed as one of the biggest moments in NASCAR history. It attracted the attention of those who had been watching that day. Soon more became fans of the sport. The Daytona 500 became an even bigger event after that day.

A New Generation

As television focused more on NASCAR after the 1979 Daytona 500, the sport experienced a shift. From 1980 to 2000, some of NASCAR's most successful drivers won the Daytona 500 for the final time.

The most notable was Richard Petty. The son of the Daytona 500's first winner scored his seventh and final Daytona 500 victory in 1981. Through 2012, no driver had won this race more often than Petty. He finished his career with a record 200 victories in NASCAR's top series (now known as the Sprint Cup Series).

Bill Elliott crosses the finish line to win the 1987 Daytona 500.

Meanwhile, new stars emerged, going faster than drivers had ever traveled around the 2.5-mile speedway. By the end of this period, the Daytona 500 also saw one of the sport's all-time best drivers rewarded by finally winning the race after having come close so often before.

Going Faster

As the years progressed, the speeds increased. Cale Yarborough was the fastest qualifier for the 1984 Daytona 500 by going 201.848 mph (324.8 km/h). It marked the first time that a car had qualified at more than 200 mph at Daytona. A car traveling 200 mph (322 km/h) will go nearly the length of a football field in one second.

Daytona Goes Hollywood

The 1990 Daytona 500 featured a 44-car starting field, but when one looks at the results, only 42 cars are listed. Why? The final two cars were shooting scenes for a movie that featured NASCAR. The movie was called "Days of Thunder" and starred Tom Cruise as a driver making his way to NASCAR. The cars, driven by professional racers, ran toward the back to avoid creating any issues for the competitors. The two cars pulled off the track early in the race after they got the footage needed for the movie.

The speeds only increased. In 1987, Bill Elliott qualified at a record 210.364 mph (338.5 km/h). That remained the fastest qualifying lap through 2012.

The sport changed in 1987. The faster cars went, the easier it was for them to fly into the air when they spun. A bad crash in 1987 at Talladega Superspeedway in Alabama forced NASCAR to make rule changes to slow the cars. The track at Talladega was a bit larger than Daytona. Bobby Allison's car blew a tire, sending it into a slide. The car spun backward and launched into the air toward the catchfence. The car slammed into the fence, shredding debris into the stands and injuring some fans.

That incident led to NASCAR slowing the cars by using a carburetor restrictor plate. The device limited the amount of air that flowed into the engine. That reduced the amount of horsepower an engine produced and how fast a car could go. Stock cars could no longer travel as fast at Daytona as Elliott went that day in 1987. That did not stop the racing from being dramatic, though.

Family Reunion

The 1988 finish featured the first father-son battle for the win. Bobby Allison raced his son Davey Allison. Before they battled for the lead, though, the race featured Petty's spectacular crash.

Petty's car spun sideways and was hit by another car. That sent Petty's car into a series of barrel rolls along the frontstretch fence. Over and over the car rolled. The hood flew off. One tire flew away. Then another. The car continued to roll. Once the car was back on the ground, it spun some more before another car plowed into it. That sent Petty's car spinning again before his wild ride ended. Petty emerged with minor injuries.

With that behind and only a few laps left in the race, Bobby Allison and Davey Allison battled for the win. Bobby Allison held on for the victory. It was the first time a father and son finished first and second in the Daytona 500. It also was Bobby Allison's third Daytona 500 victory.

A few months later, however, he was severely injured in a crash during a race at another track and lost some of his memory. Allison could no longer remember that race and that finish.

The next year, NASCAR veteran Darrell Waltrip won the Daytona 500 for the only time in his career. It came in his seventeenth start in the race. He was so happy afterward that he danced in Victory Lane as he celebrated with his team.

Streakbuster

Entering the 1994 season, Sterling Marlin had run 278 races in NASCAR's top series. He had yet to win a race. Driving for a new team in 1994, he arrived at Daytona with hopes of ending his winless drought that year. He ended it in the first race of the season. The Tennessee driver, a son of a racer, won the Daytona 500. He proved it was not a fluke. Marlin won it again in 1995. He became only the third driver through 2012 to win the Daytona 500 in back-to-back years. The other two are Hall of Fame drivers Richard Petty and Cale Yarborough.

Dale Jarrett holds off Dale Earnhardt Sr. and others as the checkered flag waves at the 1993 Daytona 500.

Determination

It appeared as if another famous driver would finally win the Daytona 500 in 1990. Dale Earnhardt Sr. led on the final lap.

Then trouble struck. He ran over a piece of debris in Turn 3 and cut a tire. Earnhardt had to slow about a mile from the finish line to avoid crashing. That allowed Derrike Cope to score the upset win. It would be one of a few times Earnhardt would see victory slip away late in the race.

The 1993 Daytona 500 was among the most famous for the finish and how CBS broadcast it. Dale Jarrett battled Earnhardt for the lead on the last lap. Jarrett's father, Ned Jarrett, was in the broadcast booth as an analyst for CBS. Broadcasters typically do not root for those they are covering. But CBS allowed Ned Jarrett to call the final lap as he cheered his son.

"Come on Dale, go baby, go," Ned Jarrett said on the broadcast to the nationwide audience watching on TV. "Come on, take 'er to the inside! . . . It's the Dale and Dale show as we come off of Turn 4. You know who I'm pulling for. It's Dale Jarrett. . . . He's going to make it! Dale Jarrett is going to win the Daytona 500!"

Earnhardt again came close to winning the Daytona 500 but fell short. He finally won the race in 1998, in his twentieth attempt.

A New Star Emerges

Jeff Gordon shocked many when he won his qualifying race for the 1993 Daytona 500 at age 21. No one had won a qualifying race for the 500 at such a young age. Gordon was just getting started. He went on to win the Daytona 500 twice in the 1990s, winning in 1997 and 1999.

In 1997, he was a part of a 1–2–3 finish by Hendrick Motorsports drivers. Teammate Terry Labonte finished second and teammate Ricky Craven placed third in that race. In 1999, Gordon made a daring move past Rusty Wallace to take the lead with 11 laps left and held on for the victory.

Gordon also won three NASCAR championships during the 1990s. He added a fourth championship in 2001 and won the Daytona 500 for a third time in 2005. He is among the most successful drivers to race at Daytona and in NASCAR.

As Earnhardt came down pit road and headed toward Victory Lane, there was a scene unlike any other before in NASCAR. Crew members from other teams stood side-by-side. They applauded Earnhardt. Some slapped his hand as he slowly drove by. It was their way of showing their respect for Earnhardt and how happy they were that he had finally won after coming so close so many times.

After Earnhardt reached Victory Lane, he climbed out of his car and stood atop the roof with his arms raised.

"Yes! Yes! Yes!" Earnhardt could be heard saying on CBS's broadcast as he climbed down off the car.

"The Daytona 500 is ours. We've won it! We've won it! We've won it!"

Crew members from many teams congratulate Dale Earnhardt Sr. in 1998 on his first Daytona 500 victory.

Tragedy Strikes

Tony Stewart's orange-and-white car turned sideways during the 2001 Daytona 500 and began a scary ride.

His car hit the backstretch wall so hard that the rear wheels came off the ground. Just then, he was hit by another car. That sent Stewart's vehicle climbing into the air. It landed on the roof of another car and continued to tumble and roll over.

Cars tried to slip by, but the track was nearly blocked. Several cars crashed into each other. Stewart's car continued rolling and landed on

Dale Earnhardt Sr.'s No. 3 car crashes into the wall on the final lap of the 2001 Daytona 500.

the hood of teammate Bobby Labonte's car. The contact ripped the hood off Labonte's car and flames shot from his engine. A total of 19 cars were involved in the accident. After Stewart's car finally stopped, he climbed out without serious injuries.

Tragic Finish

There was another multi-car crash at the end of the race. As the last lap began, Michael Waltrip led. Waltrip drove for Dale Earnhardt Sr.'s team. In second place was Earnhardt's son, Dale Earnhardt Jr. He also drove for his dad's team. Dale Earnhardt Sr. ran in third place.

Tragedy struck as the cars exited the final corner. Waltrip and Earnhardt Jr. pulled away from the pack and Waltrip won the race. Behind them, cars ran bunched together. They hit. Earnhardt Sr., running along the bottom of the track, got hit in the rear. It turned his car right and he headed up toward the Turn 4 wall. He hit nearly head-on. The car slid down the track and stopped in the infield grass near another car in the wreck.

Earnhardt Sr.'s accident did not look as severe as Stewart's crash earlier in the race, but it was. A little more than two hours later, NASCAR President Mike Helton announced: "We've lost Dale Earnhardt."

One of NASCAR's greatest drivers had died.

A Painful Win

Michael Waltrip won the 2001 Daytona 500 driving for Dale Earnhardt Sr.'s team. Earnhardt's death tempered Waltrip's feelings about that victory. Two years later, Waltrip won the Daytona 500 again. He was still driving for Earnhardt's team. This time he enjoyed the moment more than he had in 2001. Waltrip would later go on to start his own team and drive for it. As his driving career came closer to an end, he began doing more and more work on television broadcasts of NASCAR races, following the lead of his older brother, Darrell Waltrip.

Fans Mourn

It did not seem possible. Earnhardt Sr. was among the sport's most popular drivers. He was a hero to many fans.

Earnhardt grew up in the mill town of Kannapolis, North Carolina. He came from a modest family with little money. He showed what someone could be with hard work and determination.

Many fans also were attracted to his black No. 3 car. Earnhardt raced with a swagger. He was daring. He was exciting. He was known to bump the cars of other drivers out of his way. His nickname was "The Intimidator."

Fans left their caps on the fence at Turn 4 of Daytona International Speedway in tribute to the fallen Dale Earnhardt Sr. in 2001.

Fans were drawn to Earnhardt because he won many races. He won seven championships. That tied Richard Petty for most in NASCAR history.

That Earnhardt suddenly was gone saddened fans. They expressed their grief in many ways. Those at Daytona created a makeshift memorial along a fence inside Turn 4. They left Earnhardt hats, shirts, and other mementos. Fans showed up at the headquarters for Dale Earnhardt Inc., the team Earnhardt owned. First a few came, then more. Soon there were hundreds outside the North Carolina race shop. They left Earnhardt items, flowers, handwritten notes, and more. Never had the sport and its fans felt such agony.

A public memorial was shown on television. Some fans drove from several states away just to be outside the church that day. NASCAR commissioned an investigation of the accident. It lasted six months, and the official accident report was two volumes.

New Safety Measures

Earnhardt's accident sped up a safety effort NASCAR was undertaking. Numerous changes were made in an effort to keep drivers safer. No driver in the next decade died in a crash in a NASCAR Sprint Cup Series event. That success can be credited to many safety changes NASCAR created.

Richard Childress

For most of his career, Dale Earnhardt Sr. drove for Richard Childress. Earnhardt won six of his seven championships driving for Childress. They also were close friends. They often hunted and spent time together away from the racetrack.

Childress would watch as one of his drivers, Kevin Harvick, won the Daytona 500 in 2007. Childress has played a key role in the racing careers of his grandsons Austin and Ty Dillon. In 2012, Austin Dillon ran full time in the Nationwide Series, a level just below the Sprint Cup Series. In 2012, Ty Dillon ran full time in the Camping World Truck Series, two levels below the Sprint Cup Series.

NASCAR mandated crash data recorders in the cars. Those devices scientifically measure what happens to a car in a crash. That information helped series officials make the cars safer.

The head and neck support (HANS) device was another key safety improvement. The restraint system is now mandatory. The HANS device fits over the shoulders of drivers and attaches to their helmets. It prevents a driver's head and neck from lunging sharply forward or to the side in a crash. That prevents the chances of a deadly whiplash injury.

Driver seats also changed. They wrapped around a driver's body. They became stronger and absorbed more energy in a crash. That also helped drivers avoid injuries in a crash.

Among the biggest changes was the Steel And Foam Energy Reduction (SAFER) barrier. A steel barrier is placed in front of concrete walls that ring the tracks. Between the barrier and the concrete wall are foam blocks. When a car hits a SAFER barrier, the foam helps the barrier absorb the impact. That gives the driver a better chance of being uninjured in a crash.

In 2007, NASCAR debuted what was termed the "Car of Tomorrow." The car was intended to provide more protection for the driver. It provided more room for the driver. It also was designed to increase a

Jeff Gordon practices in NASCAR's new Car of Tomorrow in 2008 before a race in California.

driver's safety as much as possible. NASCAR also built a research and development center to find other ways to make drivers safer.

Dale Earnhardt Sr.'s death at NASCAR's biggest race was a shock for the sport. But fans could take some solace in the fact that his legacy helped make NASCAR much safer for future generations.

Moving Forward

It was six years to the day since his father won the Daytona 500 on the same track. And it was only three years since his father died there. Each time Dale Earnhardt Jr. circled Daytona International Speedway, he passed the spot in Turn 4 where his father's fatal crash took place.

Earnhardt Jr. had raced at this track since that day in 2001. He had even won other races there. But he had yet to win the Daytona 500.

In the days before the 2004 Daytona 500, Earnhardt Jr. talked about his frustration with never winning the race.

Dale Earnhardt Jr. races toward the finish line in first place at the 2004 Daytona 500.

DAYTONA
500
The Great American Race
FEBRUARY 15
2004

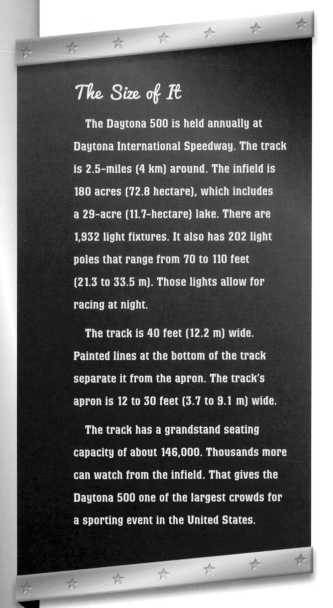

The Size of It

The Daytona 500 is held annually at Daytona International Speedway. The track is 2.5-miles (4 km) around. The infield is 180 acres (72.8 hectare), which includes a 29-acre (11.7-hectare) lake. There are 1,932 light fixtures. It also has 202 light poles that range from 70 to 110 feet (21.3 to 33.5 m). Those lights allow for racing at night.

The track is 40 feet (12.2 m) wide. Painted lines at the bottom of the track separate it from the apron. The track's apron is 12 to 30 feet (3.7 to 9.1 m) wide.

The track has a grandstand seating capacity of about 146,000. Thousands more can watch from the infield. That gives the Daytona 500 one of the largest crowds for a sporting event in the United States.

"I don't want to keep on coming close," he said. "I don't want to keep on coming close and losing. That was real tough on my family. Not only on my dad, it was hard on me just being a kid. I wanted him to win so bad without even understanding the ins and outs of the sport. I don't want to sit here 20 years later and still be coming so close I can't stand it. That's the way this place is."

Earnhardt Jr. did not have to wait 20 years like his father to win this race. The driver known by fans simply as "Junior" won the 2004 Daytona 500. He and his father became the third father-son combo to win the Daytona 500. They joined Lee and Richard Petty and Bobby and Davey Allison in that category.

Dale Earnhardt Jr. celebrates with his crew after winning the 2004 Daytona 500.

Winning the Daytona 500 is always special for a driver. It carried even more significance for Earnhardt Jr. This was the track on which his father died just three years earlier.

After he won, Earnhardt Jr. stopped his car at the start/finish line. He climbed out and saluted the crowd. Their cheers were nearly louder than the cars. His team ran to him. They hugged and celebrated. They hoisted Earnhardt Jr. on their shoulders. Before driving his car to Victory Lane, the driver did donuts in the grass.

"This is more important to me than anything," Earnhardt Jr. said later that day. "I've put a lot of emphasis on coming down here and winning this race just because of what I've been through down here."

Unforgettable Finish

One of the more spectacular finishes in the Daytona 500 came in 2007. Two cars battling for the lead raced across the finish line side-by-side. Cars crashed behind them.

Kevin Harvick went from fifth to first on the last lap. But he had to hold off Mark Martin to win the race. They ran side-by-side off the final corner of the final lap. The cars racing for third place behind them hit one another. They began to wreck. Other cars could not avoid the incident.

As Harvick and Martin raced to the finish line, more cars crashed. Harvick nipped Martin at the finish line by inches. Clint Bowyer's car was hit from behind and tipped over on to its roof. It slid across the finish line upside down and into the infield grass before turning back over. Flames shot from the engine. Bowyer emerged uninjured.

A year later, the race featured another last-lap pass for the victory. This time, there was not a crash. Tony Stewart led at the beginning of that final lap. He had won championships in NASCAR, but he had never won a Daytona 500. He was one lap from that. But he could not hold the lead.

Ryan Newman got a push from his teammate, Kurt Busch, on the backstretch to shoot into the lead. Newman won, leaving Stewart still without a Daytona 500 title.

Jimmie Johnson

Jimmie Johnson won the 2006 Daytona 500, and few could imagine what it would begin. Johnson went on to win the NASCAR Cup Series championship that year. He won the title the next year. And the next. And the next. And the next. Johnson won the championship five consecutive years. No one had ever done that before. His luck in the Daytona 500 since that 2006 win, though, has not been as good. From 2007 to 2012, Johnson did not finish better than twenty-seventh in the race.

Bizarre Crash

No Daytona 500 was like 2012. The 200-lap event had been shortened by rain only four times. But in 2012, the race was pushed back a day to Monday. Rain delayed it that day, and the race started at night. It was the first time the Daytona 500 had ever started in the evening.

The race featured one of the most bizarre accidents in the speedway's history. A caution came out on lap 158 after a car spin. Juan Pablo Montoya came to the pits to have his crew check his car during the caution. After returning to the track, he raced to catch the pack of cars behind the pace car. But a mechanical piece broke as he entered Turn 3. His car slid up the track and crashed into a jet dryer.

Hall of Fame

NASCAR created a Hall of Fame in Charlotte, North Carolina, and inducted its first five-man class in 2010. Among those selected to the Hall of Fame are some of the top drivers to race in the Daytona 500. Those Daytona 500 winning drivers in the Hall of Fame include: Richard Petty, Bobby Allison, Dale Earnhardt Sr., Junior Johnson, David Pearson, Lee Petty, Darrell Waltrip, and Cale Yarborough. They had won the Daytona 500 a combined 19 times out of the 54 times the race had been held through 2012.

Matt Kenseth holds off Dale Earnhardt Jr. (88) and Greg Biffle to win the 2012 Daytona 500 in the first year the race is held at night.

A jet dryer is a jet engine that blows extremely hot air to dry the track after it has rained. It is also used to blow debris off the track so the cars can race safely.

When Montoya's car slammed into the jet dryer, there was an explosion. Fuel spilled and ignited. A huge plume of smoke rose and soon flames engulfed the jet dryer. The driver and another worker exited the truck safely. Montoya also escaped injury. But the race had to be stopped as the jet dryer burned.

Finally, just before 1 a.m., the white flag signaled the final lap. NASCAR veteran Matt Kenseth held off Earnhardt Jr. and Greg Biffle for the win.

The 2012 race was not like anything that had ever been seen in the Daytona 500. Then again, as the history of this race has proven, there is no race quite like the Daytona 500.

TIMELINE

Bill France Sr. signs a contract with Daytona Beach, Florida, to build Daytona International Speedway on August 16.

1954

The first Daytona 500 is held on February 22. Lee Petty is declared winner three days later.

1959

In separate Daytona 500 qualifying races on February 14, Lee Petty and his son, Richard, both crash and sail over the guardrail.

1961

Ten days after pulling Marvin Panch out of his burning car, Tiny Lund wins the Daytona 500 driving for Panch's team on February 24.

1963

Richard Petty wins the first of his record seven Daytona 500s on February 23.

1964

Dale Jarrett beats Dale Earnhardt Sr. to win the Daytona 500 as Jarrett's father, Ned, calls the finish on CBS' broadcast on February 14.

1993

Earnhardt Sr. wins the Daytona 500 for the first time on February 15. It comes in his twentieth attempt.

1998

Earnhardt Sr. dies in a crash on the last corner of the last lap of the Daytona 500 on February 18.

2001

President George W. Bush serves as the Daytona 500 grand marshal on February 15. Dale Earnhardt Jr. wins.

2004

Mario Andretti wins the Daytona 500 on February 26. He later goes on to win the Indianapolis 500 and a Formula One championship.

1967

On February 17, Richard Petty becomes the first driver to win the Daytona 500 in back-to-back years.

1974

David Pearson and Richard Petty crash coming to the finish line in one of the race's most dramatic finishes on February 15. Pearson wins.

1976

CBS broadcasts the Daytona 500 live from start to finish for the first time on February 18. Richard Petty wins.

1979

Bobby Allison holds off his son Davey to win his third Daytona 500 on February 14.

1988

Jeff Gordon wins the Daytona 500 for a third time on February 20, becoming the fifth driver to win the race at least three times.

2005

NASCAR's "Car of Tomorrow" debuts. It is one of the many new safety measures adopted after Earnhardt Sr.'s death.

2007

Trevor Bayne becomes the youngest winner of the Daytona 500 at 20 years, 1 day, on February 20.

2011

Rain pushes the start of the Daytona 500 into Monday evening, making it the first night-time running of the race. Matt Kenseth wins.

2012

CHAMPIONSHIP OVERVIEW

The Trophy

The Daytona 500 winner is awarded the Harley J. Earl Trophy, named after a friend of NASCAR founder Bill France Sr. and a designer at General Motors. The winner receives a replica of the trophy. The original trophy remains on display at the track.

The Legends

Bobby Allison: Won three Daytona 500s from 1978 to 1988.

Jeff Gordon: Won three Daytona 500s from 1997 to 2005.

Dale Jarrett: Won three Daytona 500s from 1993 to 2000.

Richard Petty: Won seven Daytona 500s from 1964 to 1981.

Cale Yarborough: Won four Daytona 500s from 1968 to 1984.

The Track

Daytona International Speedway opened in 1959 and has held the Daytona 500 every year since. The Daytona 500 has kicked off NASCAR's top racing season every year since 1982. The brainchild of NASCAR founder Bill France Sr., the 2.5-mile (4 km) tri-oval with banked turns revolutionized stock car racing. Although the Daytona 500 is its most famous race, the speedway hosts several other races, stock car or otherwise, on its vast complex in central Florida.

GLOSSARY

banking
The sloping of a curved portion of a racetrack from the bottom of the track to the wall.

berm
A flat area that separates two spaces.

carburetor
A device that connects to the gas pedal that is mounted on the engine and controls the air/fuel mixture that flows into the engine.

drafting
An aerodynamic effect that allows two cars running nose-to-tail to go faster than a single car running alone.

pit
An area where pit crews service the car by changing tires, adding fuel, and making other adjustments.

pit stop
When a driver breaks from racing so the pit crew can service the car.

restrictor plate
A metal plate with four holes that restricts the airflow to the carburetor, which reduces horsepower and slows the cars. Used only at Daytona International Speedway and Talladega Superspeedway, two of the sport's biggest tracks.

series
A racing season consisting of several races.

Selected Bibliography

Bechtel, Mark. *He Crashed Me So I Crashed Him Back: The True Story Of The Year The King, Jaws, Earnhardt, And The Rest Of NASCAR'S Feudin', Fightin' Good Ol' Boys Put Stock Car Racing On The Map*. New York: Little, Brown and Company, 2010.

Hinton, Ed. *Daytona: From the Birth of Speed to the Death of the Man in Black*. New York: Warner Books, 2001.

Menzer, Joe. *The Great American Gamble: How the 1979 Daytona 500 Gave Birth to a NASCAR Nation*. Hoboken, NJ: John Wiley and Sons, 2009.

Zeller, Bob. *Daytona 500: An Official History*. Phoenix, AZ: David Bull Publishing, 2002.

Further Readings

Edelstein, Robert. *NASCAR Legends: Memorable Men, Moments, And Machines In Racing History*. New York: The Overlook Press, 2011.

Pimm, Nancy Roe. *The Daytona 500: The Thrill and Thunder of the Great American Race*. Minneapolis, MN: Millbrook Press, 2011.

Waltrip, Michael, and Ellis Henican. *In The Blink Of An Eye: Dale, Daytona and the Day that Changed Everything*. New York: Hyperion Books, 2011.

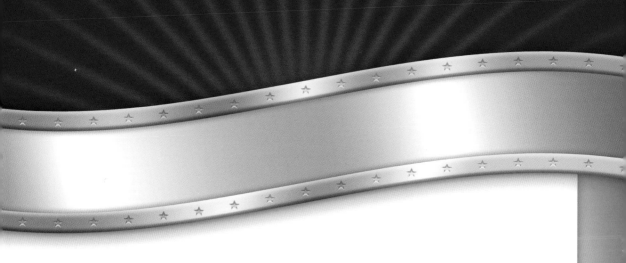

Web Links

To learn more about the Daytona 500, visit ABDO Publishing Company online at **www.abdopublishing.com**. Web sites about the Daytona 500 are featured on our Book Links page. These links are routinely monitored and updated to provide the most current information available.

Places to Visit

Daytona International Speedway
1801 W. International Speedway Blvd.
Daytona Beach, FL 32114
(877) 306-RACE (7223)
www.daytonainternationalspeedway.com
Daytona International Speedway is host to the Daytona 500 and several other racing events each season. The complex features a museum, arcade, and gift shop. Tours are available throughout the year.

NASCAR Hall of Fame
400 East Martin Luther King Blvd.
Charlotte, NC 28202
(704) 654-4400
www.nascarhall.com
This hall of fame highlights the greatest competitors and moments in NASCAR's history. The Hall features items ranging from former cars to artifacts used in competition.

INDEX

About the Author

Dustin Long is an award-winning journalist who has covered NASCAR since 1999. His work has appeared in *USA Today*, *Sports Illustrated*'s Web site SI.com, and the *New York Times*. He authored *The Petty Family Album: In Tribute to Adam Petty*. Raised in Indiana, he lives near Charlotte, North Carolina, with his wife.